Jack C. Richards & Chuck Sandy

Passages

Third Edition

T0349656

Workbook 2 A

CAMBRIDGE
UNIVERSITY PRESS

CAMBRIDGE
UNIVERSITY PRESS

University Printing House, Cambridge CB2 8BS, United Kingdom

One Liberty Plaza, 20th Floor, New York, NY 10006, USA

477 Williamstown Road, Port Melbourne, VIC 3207, Australia

314–321, 3rd Floor, Plot 3, Splendor Forum, Jasola District Centre, New Delhi – 110025, India

79 Anson Road, #06–04/06, Singapore 079906

Cambridge University Press is part of the University of Cambridge.

It furthers the University's mission by disseminating knowledge in the pursuit of education, learning and research at the highest international levels of excellence.

www.cambridge.org
Information on this title: www.cambridge.org/9781107627345

© Cambridge University Press 2015

This publication is in copyright. Subject to statutory exception and to the provisions of relevant collective licensing agreements, no reproduction of any part may take place without the written permission of Cambridge University Press.

First published 1998
Second edition 2008
Third edition 2015
Update to Third edition published 2021

Printed in Great Britain by Ashford Colour Press Ltd.

A catalogue record for this publication is available from the British Library

ISBN 978-1-009-04083-9 Student's Book 2 with eBook
ISBN 978-1-009-04084-6 Student's Book 2A with eBook
ISBN 978-1-009-04085-3 Student's Book 2B with eBook
ISBN 978-1-009-04092-1 Student's Book 2 with Digital Pack
ISBN 978-1-009-04093-8 Student's Book 2A with Digital Pack
ISBN 978-1-009-04094-5 Student's Book 2B with Digital Pack
ISBN 978-1-107-62726-0 Workbook 2
ISBN 978-1-107-62734-5 Workbook 2A
ISBN 978-1-107-62780-2 Workbook 2B
ISBN 978 1 107 62766-6 Teacher's Edition 2 with Assessment Audio
ISBN 978-1-107-62749-9 Class Audio 2
ISBN 978-1-009-04095-2 Full Contact 2 with Digital Pack
ISBN 978-1-009-04096-9 Full Contact 2A with Digital Pack
ISBN 978-1-009-04097-6 Full Contact 2B with Digital Pack
ISBN 978-1-107-62764-2 DVD 2
ISBN 978-1-107-68650-2 Presentation Plus 2

Additional resources for this publication at cambridgeone.org

Cambridge University Press has no responsibility for the persistence or accuracy of URLs for external or third-party Internet Web sites referred to in this publication and does not guarantee that any content on such Web sites is, or will remain, accurate or appropriate. Information regarding prices, travel timetables, and other factual information given in this work is correct at the time of first printing but Cambridge University Press does not guarantee the accuracy of such information thereafter.

Book design: Q2A / Bill Smith
Art direction, layout services and photo research: Tighe Publishing Services

Contents

Credits

Illustration credits

Jo Goodberry: 12
Paul Hostetler: 19, 26, 38, 49
Kim Johnson: 10, 31, 36, 55, 64
Dan McGeehan: 17, 18, 48
Koren Shadmi: 3, 20, 34, 43, 61
James Yamasaki: 41, 68

Photography credits

1 ©Photodisc/Thinkstock; **4** (*left to right*) ©Blend Images/Alamy, ©arek_malang/Shutterstock, ©Suprijono Suharjoto/Thinkstock; **5** (*clockwise from center left*) ©Fuse/Thinkstock, ©Michael Simons/Alamy, ©pcruciatti /Shutterstock, ©Dmitriy Shironosov/Thinkstock; **6** ©Catherine Yeulet/Thinkstock; **7** ©Fuse/ Thinkstock; **8** ©crystalfoto/Shutterstock; **13** ©ID1974/Shutterstock; **14** (*top to bottom*) ©Olena Mykhaylova/ iStock/Thinkstock, ©Oleksiy Mark/Thinkstock; **15** ©Stocktrek Images/Getty Images; **21** ©Flirt/SuperStock; **22** ©Photononstop/SuperStock; **23** ©BananaStock/Thinkstock; **24** ©ollyy/Shutterstock; **25** ©Khakimullin Aleksandr/Shutterstock; **27** (*top to bottom*) ©Vuk Vukmirovic/iStock/Thinkstock, ©Moviestore Collection Ltd/Alamy; **28** ©NBC/Getty Images; **30** ©CBS Photo Archive/Getty Images; **32** ©Larry Busacca/TAS/Getty Images; **35** ©Creatas/Getty Images/Thinkstock; **39** ©Cusp/SuperStock; **40** ©Tammy Hanratty/MediaBakery; **42** ©Photoshot/Hulton/Getty Images; **45** (*top to bottom*) ©Sergey Nivens/Shutterstock, ©iStock/ franckreporter, ©iStock/MachineHeadz; **47** (*left to right, top to bottom*) ©Dean Bertoncelj/iStock/Thinkstock, ©Universal/Courtesy: Everett Collection, ©Kylie McLaughlin/Lonely Planet Images/Getty Images, ©MariusdeGraf/Shutterstock, ©Blend Images/Masterfile, ©Gao lin hk/Imaginechina/AP Images; **50** (*left to right, top to bottom*) ©MustafaNC/Shutterstock, ©Dmitry Zinovyev/Shutterstock, ©e2dan/Shutterstock, ©Reinhold Leitner/Shutterstock, ©Reddogs/Shutterstock, ©Nailia Schwarz/Shutterstock, ©Sergey Goruppa/Shutterstock, ©Wendy Kaveney Photography/Shutterstock, ©Donovan van Staden/Shutterstock, ©Nantawat Chotsuwan/Shutterstock, ©Steve Byland/istock/Thinkstock, ©iStock/Sergey Goruppa; **52** ©KidStock/Blend Images/Corbis; **53** (*top to bottom*) ©Gary Crabbe/Enlightened Images/Alamy, ©Falk Kienas/istock/Thinkstock; **54** ©Eric Isselée/Thinkstock; **57** ©E+/MachineHeadz/Getty Images; **59** ©Assembly/Media Bakery; **62** (*left to right, top to bottom*) ©Pressmaster/Shutterstock, ©Olga Danylenko/ Shutterstock, ©iStock/btrenkel, ©Stockbyte/Thinkstock, ©Graham Oliver/Media Bakery, ©Andrey Yurlov/ Shutterstock; **63** © INTERFOTO/Alamy; **65** ©Jon Kopaloff/FilmMagic/Getty Images; **66** ©ZUMA Press, Inc./Alamy; **71** ©Goodluz/Shutterstock; **Back cover:** (*clockwise from top center*) ©Leszek Bogdewicz/ Shutterstock, ©Wavebreak Media/Thinkstock, ©Blend Images/Alamy, ©limpido/Shutterstock

Text credits

The authors and publishers acknowledge the following sources of copyright material and are grateful for the permissions granted. While every effort has been made, it has not always been possible to identify the sources of all the material used, or to trace all copyright holders. If any omissions are brought to our notice, we will be happy to include the appropriate acknowledgments on reprinting.

12 Adapted from "Decoding Body Language," by John Mole, 1999, http://www.johnmole.com. Reproduced with permission; **18** Adapted from "How Artificial Intelligence is Changing Our Lives," by Gregory M. Lamb. Adapted with permission from the September 16, 2012 issue of *The Christian Science Monitor*. Copyright © 2012 The Christian Science Monitor, www.CSMonitor.com; **24** Adapted from "Rumor Detectives: True Story or Online Hoax?" by David Hochman, *Reader's Digest*, April 2009. Reprinted with permission from Reader's Digest. Copyright © 2009 by The Reader's Digest Association, Inc.; **30** Adapted from an NPR news report titled "Is The 'CSI Effect' Influencing Courtrooms?" by Arun Rath, originally published on NPR.org on February 5, 2011 and used with the permission of NPR. Copyright © 2011 National Public Radio, Inc. Any unauthorized duplication is strictly prohibited; **36** Adapted from "Study Suggests Music May Someday Help Repair Brain," by Robert Lee Hotz, *Los Angeles Times*, November 9, 1998. Copyright © 1998 Los Angeles Times. Reprinted with permission; **42** Adapted from "What's the Tipping Point?" by Malcolm Gladwell. Copyright © by Malcolm Gladwell. Reprinted by permission of the author; **48** Adapted from "Sensory Ploys and the Scent of Marketing," by Robert Budden, *Financial Times*, June 3, 2013. Copyright © The Financial Times Limited 2013. All Rights Reserved; **54** Adapted from "Fairy Tale Comes True," by Alexandar S. Dragicevic, *The Toronto Star*, July 23, 1998. Copyright © Associated Press; **60** Adapted from "Does the Language you Speak Change the Way You Think?" by Kevin Hartnett, *The Boston Globe*, February 27, 2013. Reproduced with permission of Kevin Hartnett; **66** Adapted from "Tiny Grants Keep 'Awesome' Ideas Coming," by Billy Baker, *The Boston Globe*, October 10, 2011. Copyright © 2011 Boston Globe. All rights reserved. Used by permission and protected by the Copyright Laws of the United States. The printing, copying, redistribution, or retransmission of this Content without express written permission is prohibited; **72** Adapted from "The Twelve Attributes of a Truly Great Place to Work," by Tony Schwartz, *Harvard Business Review*, September 19, 2011. Reproduced with permission.

1 RELATIONSHIPS

LESSON A ▶ *The best of friends*

1 GRAMMAR

Read this paragraph from a blog post about friendship. Find the phrasal verbs and write them in the correct columns in the chart.

I have a lot of friends, but my best friend is Anna. She is one of those great friends you come by only once in a while. Anna knows how to cheer me up when I'm feeling bad, and she brings out the best in me when I'm feeling happy. Whenever I run into a problem, she always has great advice, and she usually helps me solve it. She never puts me down when I do something silly or embarrassing. I guess the thing I like best about Anna is that I can open up to her and talk about anything, like bad grades in school or family problems. I would never turn her down if she needed my help. I would stand up for her in just about any situation. I really hope that we don't drift apart in the future. I don't think I could do without her friendship!

Separable	Inseparable	Three-word verbs	Intransitive
	come by		

2 VOCABULARY

Choose the words that best complete the sentences.

1. When Mike's and Ed's ideas about art *clash* / *admire*, they argue.

2. My sister is a truly *admirable* / *beneficial* person. She works two jobs, goes to school at night, and still has time to help me with my problems.

3. Jon and Scott *empathize* / *harmonize* well as a team since they have similar working styles.

4. Kim and Emily have a truly *clashing* / *enduring* relationship. They have been best friends for more than 10 years.

5. Catherine has *benefited* / *endured* a lot from living with her grandmother, who is very understanding and a great listener.

6. Lara is good with teenagers. She is very *empathetic* / *harmonious*, really listening to their problems and helping them find their own solutions.

3 GRAMMAR

Complete these conversations with the correct form of the phrasal verbs in the box.
Use an object pronoun where needed.

cheer (someone) up	drift apart	stand up for
do without	run into	turn (someone) down

1. **A:** I'm surprised that Tom didn't support what you said in the meeting.
   I thought he agreed with you.
   B: He does agree with me, but he was afraid of what our boss would say.
   I can't believe he didn't _____*stand up for*_____ me!

2. **A:** What's wrong with Carmen? She looks so sad.
   B: I'm not sure. Let's ask her to go to lunch with us. Maybe we can
   _____.

3. **A:** Did Eric ask you to present your work at the conference next week?
   B: Yes, he did, but I _____ because I have other
   things to take care of at work.

4. **A:** Sam isn't serious about anything. I think we could really
   _____ him on our team.
   B: I agree. Let's talk to the others about it and make a decision.

5. **A:** Have you seen Yuki lately?
   B: Actually, I _____ her when I was downtown today.

6. **A:** Is it true that you and Roger aren't in touch anymore?
   B: Yes, it is. We kind of _____ when I moved to Los Angeles.

4 GRAMMAR

Complete these sentences to make them true for you.

1. Nothing cheers me up as much as _*going out to dinner with a few of my*_
   _*good friends!*_____

2. I like to hang on to friends who _____
   _____

3. When someone puts me down, I _____
   _____

4. I will stand up for anyone who _____
   _____

5. I can do without people who _____
   _____

6. I open up around people who _____
   _____

WRITING

A Read the thesis statements. Find the three best paragraph topics to support each one. Write the topics below the thesis statements.

Paragraph Topics

- ✔ Keep in touch through social media, video calls, and email.
- ✔ Be a person that your friend can trust.
- ✔ Join clubs and other organizations related to your interests or hobbies.
- ✔ Know when to give advice and when to keep silent.
- ✔ Sign up for a class, such as painting or cooking.
- ✔ Participate in community service activities, such as working with the elderly.
- ✔ Pay attention to what your friend thinks and feels.
- ✔ Get together and travel whenever possible.
- ✔ Send cards and presents for special occasions such as birthdays and holidays.

Thesis statements

1. Developing a friendship requires attention and work.

   Be a person that your friend can trust.

   _____

   _____

2. People living in big cities often have trouble making friends, but there are ways to solve this problem.

   _____

   _____

   _____

3. Maintaining a long-distance friendship is difficult, but it can be done.

   _____

   _____

   _____

B Write one additional topic for each thesis statement in part A.

1. _____

2. _____

3. _____

C Choose one of the thesis statements and write a composition. Use three paragraph topics that best support your thesis.

GRAMMAR

Read these online profiles. Underline the verb + gerund constructions, and circle the verb + infinitive constructions.

1 Naomi

My name is Naomi. I'm 30 years old, and I'm a teacher. I tend to be on the shy side, so I'm considering starting a book club so I can meet some new people. I plan to start this club as soon as possible, so email me if you're interested!

Naomi247@cup.org

2 Renee

I just moved here, and I'm looking for some new friends. I appreciate spending evenings at home cooking and listening to music. People say I tend to be kind of quiet, but I'm fun once you know more about me. If you enjoy sharing recipes, email me.

Renee8334@cup.org

3 Alex

I'm Alex Ramirez, an engineering student at National University. I really enjoy biking. Can I suggest starting a bikers' meet-up group? I'm considering entering a race, and therefore, I intend to start riding my bike every day. I hope others will join me!

alex.ramirez@cup.org

GRAMMAR

Complete the questions using the gerund or infinitive form of the verbs. Note that one of the constructions uses the passive voice. Then answer the questions and give reasons.

1. Do you get annoyed when friends ask _____*to borrow*_____ (borrow) your clothes?
   No, I don't get annoyed because I know my friends will return the clothes.

2. Would you give up _____ (practice) an instrument or sport if you got to spend more time with friends?
   _____

3. Would you refuse _____ (go out) with a friend if he or she wanted to see a movie you weren't interested in seeing?
   _____

4. Do you expect _____ (invite) every time your best friend goes out?
   _____

5. Which friend do you prefer _____ (hang out) with the most?
   _____

6. When a friend treats you to lunch, do you enjoy _____ (go) to a casual restaurant or a more formal one?
   _____

7. Would you continue _____ (talk) to a friend if he or she never answered your texts or emails?
   _____

3 VOCABULARY

Choose the words that best complete the sentences.

1. Maria and Emma *rekindled* / *resurfaced* their friendship after drifting apart from each other for many years.

2. Good friends are impossible to *replace* / *resurface*. They share so many of our memories.

3. Too much damage has been done to Al and Sam's friendship to *redefine* / *rebuild* it.

4. I can't *rehash* / *recall* the name of my tenth-grade English teacher.

5. Tim has *reconnected* / *redefined* his outlook on life. He's more optimistic now.

6. Don't bring that subject up again. I don't want to *rehash* / *rebuild* it with you.

7. After studying for the exam for two days, Cara *redefined* / *resurfaced* to eat dinner with her family.

8. I'm glad I came home for spring break. I've been *recalling* / *reconnecting* with friends that I haven't seen since last summer.

4 GRAMMAR

Imagine your friend is coming to visit you for the weekend. Write sentences describing some possible activities you can do together. Use the cues and the gerund or infinitive form of the verbs.

1. plan / take a walk somewhere nice

We should plan to take a walk
somewhere nice.

2. suggest / relax at a cozy café

_____

_____

3. consider / go to a club

_____

_____

4. prefer / get tickets to a concert

_____

_____

A Read the article. Find the words in boldface that match the definitions.

1. causes _____*spurs*_____
2. thin _____
3. annoying reminders _____
4. a good indication of _____
5. more commonly affected by _____
6. take care of and engage socially _____

Your FRIENDS & Your HEALTH «

"You're not what you eat – you're who you eat with," wrote *Scientific American*'s Christie Nicholson, reporting on research examining why our friends' weight influences our own. The study found that overweight students were more likely to lose weight if they hung out with **lean** friends – **a clear nod to** the influence of our social networks on our waistlines. But helping you lose weight isn't the only way your friends can affect you. Here are some other ways friends are good for our health:

FRIENDS GET YOU MOVING Research has found that something you might expect from your family – **nagging** – can actually work when it's coming from a pal pushing you to move more. Also, working out with a friend has the added benefit of keeping you committed to your workout plan. There's no rolling over to hit the snooze button on that early morning run if someone's waiting for you to show up!

FRIENDS KEEP YOU RELAXED Talking with friends really can help you get through troublesome times. Women in particular may be **predisposed to** the calming benefits of friendship. Researchers found that women release the hormone oxytocin when stressed, which encourages **"tend and befriend"** behavior, the *San Francisco Chronicle* reported. Chatting with friends when stressed **spurs** the release of more oxytocin, which can have a calming effect.

FRIENDS KEEP YOUR HEART HEALTHY Perhaps because they help us relax, friends are also good for the heart. Stronger social ties in general seem to lower blood pressure, which helps the heart. Married men, for example, seem to experience a particular boost in heart health, WebMD reported.

FRIENDS HELP YOU LIVE LONGER In an analysis of 148 studies, researchers found that people with stronger relationships had a 50 percent greater chance of long-term survival than those with weaker social networks. It's not quite as simple as connecting with friends and, poof, you're guaranteed to live to 100, but there is a significant body of research linking strong social ties to a longer lifespan.

B Choose the statements that are supported by information in the article.

☐ 1. Men don't seem to benefit from the relaxing effects of friendship.

☐ 2. The eating habits and lifestyle of our friends can have an influence on our own health.

☐ 3. Making plans to exercise with a friend increases the likelihood that you will.

☐ 4. Having strong social ties does not seem to have an effect on women's blood pressure.

☐ 5. Evidence suggests that strong social ties can lead to a longer life.

2 CLOTHES AND APPEARANCE

LESSON **A** ▶ *The way we dress*

GRAMMAR

Match the two parts of each sentence to tell the story of Mimi, a fashion designer.

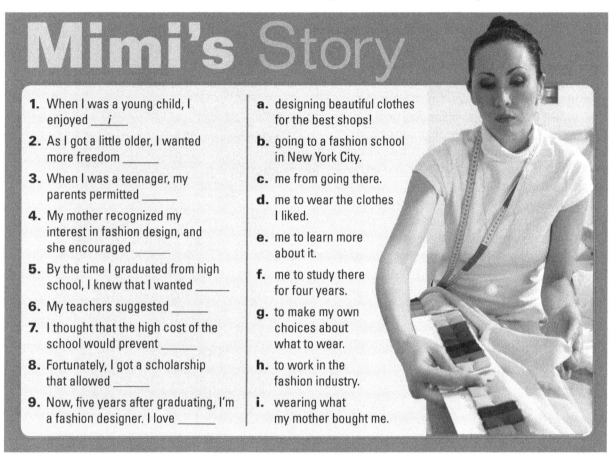

Mimi's Story

1. When I was a young child, I enjoyed ___*i*___
2. As I got a little older, I wanted more freedom _____
3. When I was a teenager, my parents permitted _____
4. My mother recognized my interest in fashion design, and she encouraged _____
5. By the time I graduated from high school, I knew that I wanted _____
6. My teachers suggested _____
7. I thought that the high cost of the school would prevent _____
8. Fortunately, I got a scholarship that allowed _____
9. Now, five years after graduating, I'm a fashion designer. I love _____

a. designing beautiful clothes for the best shops!
b. going to a fashion school in New York City.
c. me from going there.
d. me to wear the clothes I liked.
e. me to learn more about it.
f. me to study there for four years.
g. to make my own choices about what to wear.
h. to work in the fashion industry.
i. wearing what my mother bought me.

VOCABULARY

Choose the words that best complete the sentences.

1. People read fashion magazines to learn about the *sloppy* / *stylish* new clothing for each season.

2. If you are planning to go to a fancy club, wear something *chic* / *functional*.

3. Marco's *conservative* / *quirky* suit was appropriate for his interview at the bank.

4. Many teenagers think adults wear unimaginative, *fashionable* / *stuffy* clothing.

5. When I'm alone at home, I can wear *formal* / *sloppy* clothes if I want.

6. I can't understand why some people wear *retro* / *trendy* clothes from decades ago – they're so old-fashioned!

7. When I'm gardening, I wear *flashy* / *functional* jeans and a T-shirt.

8. Pop stars often wear *trendy* / *frumpy* clothes on stage.

GRAMMAR

Read the blog post about clothes and fashion. Use the gerund or the infinitive form of the verbs in parentheses.

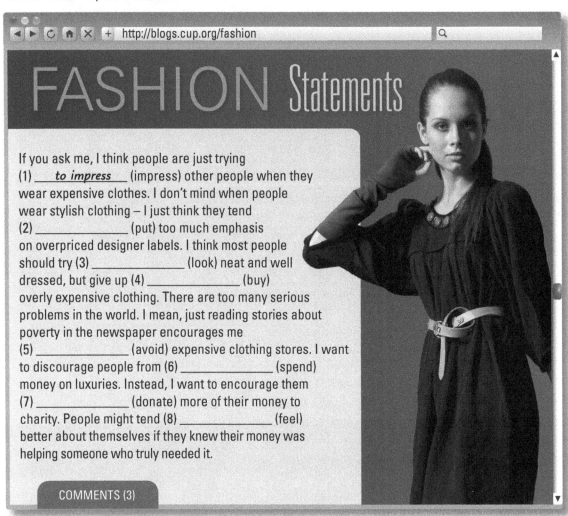

FASHION Statements

If you ask me, I think people are just trying
(1) __to impress__ (impress) other people when they
wear expensive clothes. I don't mind when people
wear stylish clothing – I just think they tend
(2) _____ (put) too much emphasis
on overpriced designer labels. I think most people
should try (3) _____ (look) neat and well
dressed, but give up (4) _____ (buy)
overly expensive clothing. There are too many serious
problems in the world. I mean, just reading stories about
poverty in the newspaper encourages me
(5) _____ (avoid) expensive clothing stores. I want
to discourage people from (6) _____ (spend)
money on luxuries. Instead, I want to encourage them
(7) _____ (donate) more of their money to
charity. People might tend (8) _____ (feel)
better about themselves if they knew their money was
helping someone who truly needed it.

COMMENTS (3)

GRAMMAR

Complete these sentences to make them true for you.

1. I don't mind wearing clothes that _are handed down to me from my brothers_
   or cousins.

2. I hate to wear clothes that _____
   _____

3. I love to wear clothes that _____
   _____

4. When I'm shopping for clothes, I enjoy _____
   _____

5. When getting dressed for a night out, I tend _____
   _____

WRITING

A Underline the thesis statements in these introductory paragraphs. Then complete each paragraph that follows with examples supporting each thesis statement.

There are many reasons for getting dressed up. Yet many of my friends seem to despise wearing anything but jeans and T-shirts. Personally, I look forward to opportunities to put on my best clothes and like to dress nicely for many different types of occasions.

There are many advantages to dressing nicely. For example, _____

_____

_____

_____

_____

Young people spend a significant portion of their income on the "right clothes." Following the newest trends in an effort to fit in can become an obsession, and keeping up with the latest fashions can be an expensive pursuit. I feel that young people need to reject the pressure to dress stylishly.

Young people should be aware that fashion magazines and blogs do not always set a good example. That is, _____

_____

_____

_____

B Choose one of these topics to write about. Then choose one of the verbs to make the thesis statement express your point of view.
1. There *are / aren't* many advantages to dressing casually at work.
2. Students *should / shouldn't* be required to wear school uniforms.
3. People *should / shouldn't* be judged by what they wear.

C Make a list of examples that support your thesis statement.

_____

_____

_____

D Use your thesis statement and examples to write a composition containing an introductory paragraph and at least two supporting paragraphs.

GRAMMAR

Read the email and underline the cleft sentences.

> To: beth234@mail.cup.org
> Subject: Kyle's visit
>
> Dear Beth,
>
> Guess what! My brother Kyle visited me yesterday. I hadn't seen him in a year. What I noticed first was the three inches he grew. He looks so tall now!
>
> He wanted to go out for lunch, so we went to my favorite café. We talked for a while. What struck me most about him was how grown up he sounded. He told me that he's doing well in school and that he has a part-time job at a supermarket – and he's even been saving money for college.
>
> After lunch, we walked through the park. Then he had to leave, but before he did, he gave me a big hug and promised to visit me again. What I realized at the end of the visit was that I have a really terrific brother!
>
> Love, Erica

GRAMMAR

Read what each person thought about Gina Riccardi, a model who visited an advertising agency. Then complete the conversation using cleft sentences with *admired, liked, noticed,* or *struck me*.

Jin: She's as beautiful in person as she is in her ads.

Brian: She is gorgeous, but (1) _what I noticed first was how relaxed and friendly she seems_.

Dolores: That's true, but (2) _____.

How about you, Jin?

Jin: Yes, her eyes are stunning, but (3) _____.

Ted: As for me, (4) _____.

Brian: You're right. Her voice is very expressive. Actually, I hear she's about to act in her first movie.

VOCABULARY

Choose the words in the box that best complete the sentences.

arrogant	eccentric	intense	sympathetic
dignified	intellectual	sinister	trustworthy

1. People think Ryan is strange and _____*eccentric*_____ because he lives with 12 cats.

2. The villain was so _____ that I shivered with fear.

3. Jonathan is so _____. He thinks he's better than everyone in the office.

4. If you need a _____ person to talk to, try Maya. She's very understanding.

5. Don't count on David to keep any secrets. He's not very _____.

6. Jiro was very _____ during the debate. He clearly has strong opinions about the topic!

7. Keri is so _____. She could be a college professor!

8. Despite all the reporters shouting questions at her, the politician remained calm and _____, not showing that she was upset at all.

GRAMMAR

Imagine you are moving to a town where you don't know anyone. What personal characteristics do you look for in potential friends? Use your own ideas to complete these sentences.

1. What I look for in a friend is *a sincere interest in other people and* _____
   a sympathetic personality. _____

2. What I think is most important is _____
   _____

3. What I probably notice first is _____
   _____

4. What I pay attention to is _____
   _____

5. What I try to find out about a new friend first is _____
   _____

6. What I think is least important is _____
   _____

5 READING

A Read the article quickly. Which of these behaviors apply to each body language type?

	Willing to listen	Not willing to listen	Engaged in conversation	Not engaged in conversation
1. responsive	☐	☐	☐	☐
2. reflective	☐	☐	☐	☐
3. combative	☐	☐	☐	☐
4. fugitive	☐	☐	☐	☐

Understanding BODY LANGUAGE

In European and North American cultures, body language behaviors can be divided into two groups: open/closed and forward/back.

Open/closed postures are the easiest to recognize. People are open to messages when they show open hands, face you fully, and have both feet on the ground. This indicates that they are willing to listen to what you have to say, even if they are disagreeing with you. When people are closed to messages, they have their arms folded or their legs crossed, and they may turn their bodies away. What this body language usually means is that people are rejecting your message.

Forward/back behavior reveals an active or a passive reaction to what is being said. If people lean forward with their bodies toward you, they are actively engaged in your message. They may be accepting or rejecting it, but their minds are on what you are saying. On the other hand, if people lean back in their chairs or look away from you, or perform activities such as drawing or cleaning their eyeglasses, you know that they are either passively taking in your message or that they are ignoring it. In either case, they are not very engaged in the conversation.

The chart below shows how these types of body language can suggest the general mental state of the listener.

OPEN

RESPONSIVE:
The person is willing to listen to you (open) and wants to participate in the conversation (forward).

REFLECTIVE:
The person is willing to listen (open) but not to share his or her opinion (back). He or she wants more time to think.

FORWARD — BACK

COMBATIVE:
There is risk of an argument. The person is engaged in the conversation (forward) but rejects your message (closed).

FUGITIVE:
The person is trying to avoid the conversation. He or she does not want to be a part of the conversation (back) and is rejecting your message (closed).

CLOSED

B Write the body language type under each picture.

responsive
reflective
combative
fugitive

1. _____   2. _____   3. _____   4. _____

3 SCIENCE AND TECHNOLOGY
LESSON A ▶ *Good science, bad science*

1 GRAMMAR

Choose the sentences that use articles incorrectly, and then rewrite them.

☑ 1. For some people, using an abacus is an alternative to using calculator.

For some people, using an abacus is an
alternative to using a calculator.

☐ 2. Abacus is the earliest form of mechanical computing.

_____

☐ 3. The abacus was invented more than 4,000 years ago.

_____

☐ 4. It consists of wires strung across wooden frame.

_____

☐ 5. An abacus can have up to 13 wires. On wires are beads, which represent units.

_____

☐ 6. Calculations are made by moving the beads up and down the wires.

_____

☐ 7. Skilled operator can make calculations on it very quickly.

_____

2 VOCABULARY

Choose the words in the box that best complete the sentences.

audacious	frivolous	problematic	unethical
confidential	hazardous	prudent	

1. Some people consider cosmetic surgery harmful and a/an _____*frivolous*_____ waste of money when not done for serious health reasons.

2. Curing cancer is still a/an _____ issue for scientists.

3. In some countries, doctors must keep medical records _____. They are forbidden to share information, even with family members.

4. Some people get sick due to improper storage or disposal of _____ materials like chemicals and poisons.

5. It's illegal and _____ to download music without permission.

6. It would take _____ actions to go against our boss's plans.

7. It would be _____ to review the contract with a lawyer before signing it. Don't put yourself at risk by making a bad deal.

3 GRAMMAR

Complete the text with *a*, *an*, or *the*. Write an *X* where an article is not required.

Digital **Cameras**

Since the early 1990s, (1) __*the*__ digital camera has changed the way we take (2) _____ pictures.

Traditional film cameras worked by focusing (3) _____ image onto light-sensitive film in the camera. To see the pictures, you had to send (4) _____ film to (5) _____ company that processed it. This was (6) _____ process that could take several hours.

Of course, digital cameras don't use film. Rather, they convert light entering the camera into (7) _____ information that can be read by (8) _____ computer. One advantage of this process is that you can see (9) _____ images immediately.

Another advantage is that you can delete (10) _____ pictures you don't like, and you can improve (11) _____ image by using special software. Of course, this can be (12) _____ disadvantage, too, since it's nearly impossible to tell just from looking whether a photo is real or not.

4 GRAMMAR

Write a sentence about each topic.

- the most helpful kind of technology
- the trendiest product on the market
- the silliest invention
- a medical cure I'd like to see discovered
- the most interesting website

1. *I think the most helpful kind of technology is the solar panel, which can provide electricity without producing much harmful waste.*

2. _____
    _____

3. _____
    _____

4. _____
    _____

5. _____
    _____

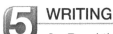

A Read the article. Underline the main information in each paragraph that would belong in a summary.

ASTEROID MINING

One day in the not-so-distant future, small robotic spaceships will search the inner solar system mapping asteroids and determining which to harvest. Those asteroids containing valuable resources like iron, nickel, hydrogen, and reusable water will then be mined by larger robotic spacecrafts or turned into space-based manufacturing centers.

Robotically controlled factories built on asteroids will turn space rock water into rocket fuel and asteroid metals into everything needed for space-based manufacturing. Given the possibly endless supply of resource-rich asteroids, the pioneers of asteroid mining will become incredibly wealthy as they lead us into a new age of space development. At least, that's the plan.

Although it may sound like science fiction, big investors are already taking such ideas seriously enough to put substantial money into asteroid mining and space exploration companies. NASA, the U.S. space agency, is enthusiastic. In fact,

NASA sees these plans as the first step toward colonizing space. By locating manufacturing facilities and rocket fueling stations on asteroids already in space, costs will be reduced and long journeys into space will become possible. This will make human colonization of other parts of the solar system a real possibility.

Before we get too excited, though, it's important to remember that most of the technology needed to mine asteroids and build orbital factories doesn't exist yet. Still, early investors and the companies they're investing in believe they will be successful and that along the way the asteroid-mining technologies they develop will help bring about a new age.

B Choose the sentence in each pair that could belong in a summary of the article.

1. ☐ There is a great deal of serious interest in mining asteroids for their valuable resources.

 ☐ Many asteroids contain valuable resources such as iron and nickel.

2. ☐ NASA feels asteroid mining could make space colonization possible.

 ☐ Asteroid mining could lead to a new era of space exploration and colonization.

C Now, write a summary of the article by rewriting the main points in your own words.

_____

_____

_____

_____

_____

_____

_____

_____

_____

_____

GRAMMAR

Read the sentences. Choose whether the *-ing* clause implies actions that happened at the same time, at a different time, or for a reason. Sometimes more than one answer is possible.

	Same time	Different time	Reason
1. Having recently learned how to text, my grandmother now sends me several messages a day!	☐	☑	☑
2. Being a prudent consumer, I did some research before I bought my laptop.	☐	☐	☐
3. While going to the birthday party, I got lost.	☐	☐	☐
4. Having lost my ATM card, I can't withdraw money from an ATM.	☐	☐	☐
5. Having downloaded a new video calling app, I can call friends anywhere in the world for free.	☐	☐	☐
6. Zoe is in her room watching movies on her tablet.	☐	☐	☐
7. Having had trouble programming my home security system, I now ask my wife to program it for us.	☐	☐	☐

GRAMMAR

Write sentences using the cues and an *-ing* clause.

1. *Same time:* Lily / break her digital camera / take a picture

   Lily broke her digital camera taking a picture.

   Taking a picture, Lily broke her digital camera.

2. *Different time:* Diego / watch a show about alternative energy / buy an electric car

   _____

3. *Reason:* Bella / be a resourceful person / build her own computer

   _____

4. *Different time:* Dan / injure his arm / receive a bone scan

   _____

5. *Same time:* Celia / be in her car / listen to satellite radio

   _____

6. *Reason:* Ken / be an eco-conscious person / always recycles his old electronics

   _____

3 VOCABULARY

Match the clauses to make logical sentences.

1. Anita is fed up with Tyler __c__
2. Children are reliant on their parents ____
3. Julia is grateful for all the help ____
4. Make sure you are familiar with ____
5. I'm curious about ____
6. People are intimidated by George, ____
7. Gwen is so crazy about cooking ____
8. I've been suspicious of Ryan ____

a. she got from friends while she was ill.
b. ever since I saw him holding my phone.
c. because he asks too many questions.
d. that she opened her own restaurant.
e. but he's actually nicer than he looks!
f. to feed, shelter, and clothe them until they're grown.
g. what happens next on my favorite TV show.
h. the program before using it in your next presentation.

4 GRAMMAR

Have you had good or bad experiences doing the activities in the box or similar activities using technology? Write sentences about your experience using *-ing* clauses.

> using a video streaming service
> learning how to use a new cell phone
> creating a social networking profile
> shopping online

1. _Having signed up for a new video streaming service, I realized it didn't offer all the movies I wanted to see._

2. _____

3. _____

4. _____

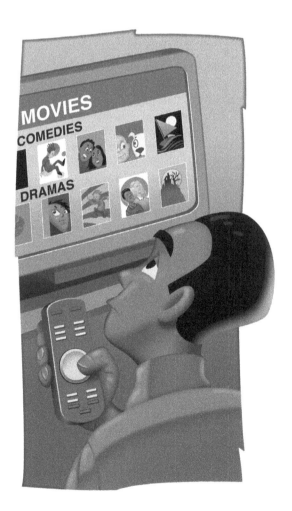

A What does *mundanely ubiquitous* mean? Read the article and choose the answer.

☐ unsurprisingly common   ☐ amazingly rare

ARTIFICIAL INTELLIGENCE
IN OUR LIVES

From the Curiosity space probe that landed on Mars without human help, to the cars whose dashboards we can now talk to, to smartphones that talk back to us, so-called artificial intelligence (AI) is changing our lives – sometimes in ways that are obvious and visible, but often in subtle and invisible forms.

AI is making Internet searches quicker, translating texts from one language to another, and recommending a better route through traffic. It helps detect fraudulent patterns in credit-card searches and tells us when we've crossed over the center line while driving. Even your toaster is about to join the AI revolution. You'll put a bagel in it, take a picture with your smartphone, and the phone will send the toaster all the information it needs to brown the bread perfectly.

In a sense, AI has become almost **mundanely ubiquitous,** from the intelligent sensors that adjust the settings in digital cameras, to the heat and humidity probes in dryers, to the automatic parking feature in cars. And more applications for AI are coming out of labs and laptops by the hour. "It's an exciting world," says

Colin Angle, cofounder of a company that has created a robotic vacuum cleaner that uses AI to navigate its way around furniture.

What may be most surprising about AI today, in fact, is how little amazement it creates. Perhaps science-fiction stories with humanlike androids – from the charming Data in *Star Trek*, to the obedient C-3PO in *Star Wars*, to the sinister Terminator in the similarly named series of movies – have raised unrealistic expectations. Or maybe human nature just doesn't stay amazed for long.

"Today's mind-popping, eye-popping technology in 18 months will be as blasé and old as a 1980s pair of double-knit trousers," says Paul Saffo, who analyzes trends to predict the future. "Our expectations are a moving target." If voice-recognition programs in smartphones had come out in 1980, "it would have been the most astonishing, breathtaking thing," he says. But by the time they arrived, "we were so used to other things going on we said, 'Oh, yeah, no big deal.' Technology goes from magic to invisible-and-taken-for-granted in about two nanoseconds."

B For each pair of sentences, choose the one the author would agree with.

1. ☐ a. AI has become so integrated into technology that most people are unaware of it.
   ☐ b. AI is making some aspects of daily life more complicated than necessary.

2. ☐ a. People are surprised that AI is even better than their expectations from movies.
   ☐ b. People aren't amazed by AI because of their high expectations from movies.

3. ☐ a. Technology advances so quickly that it creates astonishment.
   ☐ b. Technology advances so rapidly that people don't stay impressed by it for long.

4. ☐ a. It's likely we'll quickly see an increasing number of new applications for AI.
   ☐ b. It's unlikely that there will be many new developments in AI.

4 SUPERSTITIONS AND BELIEFS

LESSON A ▶ *Superstitions*

 VOCABULARY

Match the phrases to make logical sentences.

1. I got into the best dorm on campus due to the __*e*__
2. Muriel had never bowled before, so her high score was ____
3. I tried to get tickets to the play, but I couldn't. I was ____
4. Before Max went off to college, I wished him the ____
5. Celia drives too fast. One day she's going to have an accident. I wish she wouldn't ____
6. I was hoping to get more information about the job, but ____
7. Jim's car was broken into twice in one week. He's had some really ____

a. push her luck.
b. bad luck.
c. best of luck.
d. out of luck.
e. luck of the draw.
f. beginner's luck.
g. no such luck.

 GRAMMAR

Underline the reporting clauses in this passage.

Fact OR Fiction?

Some ideas have been repeated so often that we just accept them as facts. <u>When someone asserts that</u> you can see the Great Wall of China from outer space, do we ask for proof? Probably not. But if you speak to anyone who's looked closely at photos of the earth taken from the moon, they'll sometimes admit that they can't find a trace of the Great Wall. And if people argue that you can badly hurt someone with a coin dropped from a very tall structure, we assume it must be true. Others have claimed that it's true many times before, right? However, experts agree that there's really no need to worry, and they report that a dropped coin could not reach a high enough speed to cause any real damage. One more case: Do you ever doubt that we, as humans, have only five senses? Not likely. Yet, apart from sight, smell, taste, and so on, some scientists explain that many other senses are in play: balance, movement, time, and hunger among them. However, there isn't much agreement about the total number, so maybe we should accept that there are five basic senses and leave the rest open to <u>Continue</u> . . .

Combine each pair of sentences using the words in parentheses.

1. As a child, I believed some strange things. A monster was living under my bed. (believe)

   As a child, I ____*believed (that)*____ a monster *was living under my bed*.

2. To keep the monster away, I had to do certain things. I had to adjust the covers over me. (feel)

   To keep the monster away, I _____
   I _____.

3. I needed extra protection. My teddy bear would help me. (assume)

   I _____ my teddy bear
   _____.

4. I was fairly sure of one thing. My parents wouldn't believe me. (doubt)

   I _____ my parents
   _____.

Use the verbs in parentheses to explain what you think these people would do in the following situations.

1. Anna's friend won't travel on Friday the 13th because he considers it to be an unlucky day. Anna disagrees. How do you think Anna would reassure him? (explain)

   Anna would explain that Friday the 13th is just like any other day.

2. Luke's soccer teammate saw him rubbing a charm for good luck. How would Luke explain this? (admit)

   _____

3. Farah isn't superstitious, but her friend claims that following some superstitions brings good luck. How do you think Farah would respond? (argue)

   _____

5 WRITING

A Read the text and answer the questions. Write the letter of the appropriate sentence.

1. Which sentence is the thesis statement? _____
2. Which sentence gives general examples? _____
3. Which sentence reflects the author's personal opinion about traditional beliefs? _____
4. Which sentence restates the thesis statement? _____

Traditional Beliefs

a Traditional beliefs are not the same as superstitions. They differ in that they supposedly transmit useful information from one generation to another. **b** For example, I'm sure most of us can remember our parents telling us to eat certain foods or to avoid specific behaviors. Is there wisdom in these teachings, or are they without value? **c** Some beliefs passed down through generations reflect current medical thinking, whereas others have not passed the test of time.

Did your mother ever tell you to eat your carrots because they're good for your eyes? Well, the truth is carrots contain high levels of vitamin A. Research has linked vitamin A deficiencies to vision problems in low light, so in this sense, eating plenty of carrots actually is good for your eyes. And is garlic really good for you? It turns out that it is. Eating garlic on a regular basis can reduce the risk of serious illness and detoxify the body. How about chicken soup? We now understand that chicken contains an amino acid that is similar to a drug often prescribed for people with respiratory infections.

Unfortunately, not all of mom's advice has withstood medical inquiry. For example, generations of children have been told not to go swimming for an hour after eating. But research suggests that there is no danger in having lunch and then diving back into the ocean. Is chocolate really bad for you? Well, no, not if it's dark chocolate. Researchers now understand that dark chocolate contains enough antioxidants to make small amounts of it a healthy choice. Are fresh fruit juices really better for you than sodas? Well, yes and no. Fruit juices can contain as much sugar as soda, and both can contribute to weight gain and tooth decay. The best drink of all is simply water.

d Even though science can persuade us that some of our traditional beliefs don't hold water, there is still a lot of wisdom in the beliefs that have been handed down from generation to generation. **e** After all, much of this lore has been accumulated from thousands of years of trial-and-error experience in family healthcare. **f** We should respect this informal body of knowledge even as we search for clear scientific evidence to prove it to be true or false.

B Write a composition about traditional beliefs in your own culture. Include some you think are true and some you think are not true. Be sure to restate the thesis statement from your first paragraph in the last paragraph.

GRAMMAR

Read the article and underline the reporting verbs that are in the passive voice.

A Famous HOAX

On October 30, 1938, perhaps the most famous broadcast in the history of radio took place. Heard all over the United States, the broadcast reported that a spacecraft from Mars had landed in a small town in New Jersey. It <u>was said</u> that the Martians were attacking the surrounding area with a deadly "heat ray." Radio reporters also claimed that huge war machines had emerged from the spacecraft. After much destruction, it was announced that the Martians were dying. Specialists suggested that the Martians had no resistance to earth's infectious diseases.

Of course, this story was just a radio play, based on the novel *War of the Worlds* by H. G. Wells and directed and performed by Orson Welles. However, it is generally claimed that many people believed it, and it was reported that there was widespread panic throughout the country, especially in New Jersey. While it was not the intention of the broadcast to frighten people, its effects were widespread and dramatic. It has been suggested that Welles's broadcast offers many lessons about how the mass media can affect people in their daily lives.

Orson Welles

VOCABULARY

Cross out the word that does not fit the meaning of the sentence.

1. It is *conceivable* / ~~*misleading*~~ / *plausible* that many lowland areas will be under water if the current trend in climate change continues.

2. Fad diets that promise you'll lose 10 pounds the first day sound *convincing* / *fishy* / *far-fetched* to me. There's no way you can lose 10 pounds in one day!

3. Beware of *dubious* / *phony* / *well-founded* emails that ask you to supply personal information like your credit card number or your salary.

4. Greta gave such a(n) *believable* / *convincing* / *iffy* performance in the play that I almost forgot she was acting!

5. Stephanie's blog is *misleading* / *fishy* / *believable*. Her profile says she's 24, but I know for a fact she's only 18.

6. That Carl is a chef seems *far-fetched* / *dubious* / *conceivable* to me. The food he cooked for dinner was awful.

7. I don't believe that "all-natural" foods are better for you. Show me a *plausible* / *dubious* / *well-founded* article that proves it, and then maybe I'll believe it.

8. When Kay told me she found a great used car online, it sounded *iffy* / *far-fetched* / *credible* to me. But the car is actually pretty nice!

③ GRAMMAR

Rewrite these sentences with the words in parentheses. Use a reporting clause in the passive with *it*.

1. More than two billion people use the Internet. (estimate)

   It is estimated (that) more than two billion people use the Internet.

2. Fingernails grow faster on the hand that you use the most. (report)

   _____

3. The oldest living tree on earth is nearly 5,000 years old. (say)

   _____

4. In a baby's first year of life, parents lose between 400 and 750 hours of sleep. (believe)

   _____

5. Items like plastic cups and bags take between 500 and 1,000 years to break down. (explain)

   _____

6. About 100 hairs fall from a person's head each day. (claim)

   _____

④ GRAMMAR

Use the cues to write sentences with a reporting clause in the passive.

1. say / 15 minutes of exercise per day / may extend your life by three years

   It is said (that) 15 minutes of exercise per

   day may extend your life by three years.

2. report / the average American child / watches 20,000 commercials each year

   _____

   _____

3. suggest / traditional treatments such as acupuncture / are effective

   _____

   _____

4. claim / a cure for certain types of cancer / will be found soon

   _____

   _____

5. believe / some animals / can predict earthquakes

   _____

   _____

5 READING

A Read the article quickly to find the answers to these questions.

1. When did the Mikkelsons begin Snopes.com? _____

2. How many people visit the website each month? _____

3. What is the mission of Snopes.com? _____

RUMOR DETECTIVES

A few years ago, a woman and her husband were coming home from a ski trip when they spotted a disabled car on the side of the road. It was raining, and the driver looked distressed, so they stopped and helped him fix his flat tire. The man was extremely grateful but didn't have any cash to reward them, so he took down their personal information. A week later, the couple got a call from their bank saying their mortgage had been paid and $10,000 deposited into their account by an appreciative Bill Gates.

"Ah, the grateful millionaire," says Barbara Mikkelson with a satisfied grin.

Barbara and her husband, David, run Snopes.com, the Internet's preeminent resource for verifying and debunking rumors, ridiculous claims, and email chain letters. Whether it's an urban legend like the Gates story, an overblown warning about the latest computer virus, or that bizarre photo circulating of "Hercules, the world's biggest dog," chances are Snopes has checked it out and rated it as "true," "false," or "undetermined."

What began in 1995 as a hobby for a pair of amateur folklorists has grown into one of the Internet's most trusted authorities – and a full-time profession for the Mikkelsons. Each month, millions of people visit Snopes.com. Even the word *Snopes* has gone viral – as in, "Why didn't you Snopes that junk before forwarding it to your entire email list?"

"It's not easy to find out if these things are true or not, so people turn to us," David says.

A passion for nosing around is what brought the Mikkelsons together, and it's still their prime motivation, though their work is more than just a labor of love. The couple now earns a "very healthy" income, David says, from advertising on the site.

Though the Mikkelsons are established figures on the Web, they still prefer old-fashioned research – scouring vintage catalogs, thumbing through four newspapers a day – over finding quick answers online. David admits, however, that he might use Google or Wikipedia as a starting point.

B Are these statements true (*T*), false (*F*), or is the information not given (*NG*) in the article? Write the correct letters.

_____ 1. The Mikkelsons are now millionaires because of their work on Snopes.com.

_____ 2. Snopes.com gets hundreds of stories a day that are as far-fetched as "the grateful millionaire" one.

_____ 3. The Mikkelsons never resort to using online sources to check dubious facts.

_____ 4. The word *Snopes* is sometimes used as a verb by people familiar with the site.

_____ 5. Snopes receives income from ads placed by major international corporations.

5 MOVIES AND TELEVISION
LESSON A ▶ *Movies*

 VOCABULARY

Choose the words that best complete the sentences.

1. I love movies that are so *predictable* / (*riveting*) that you completely lose track of the time.

2. The last movie I saw wasn't original at all. In fact, it seemed pretty *formulaic* / *touching* to me.

3. The critics were disappointed with the director's new film. They said his work was unoriginal and *moving* / *mediocre*.

4. The heartbreaking relationship between the two main characters in this movie is beautiful and *predictable* / *touching*.

5. That movie was so *clichéd* / *engrossing* that I honestly forgot I was in my living room.

6. After seeing the *inspiring* / *predictable* story of a woman who set up an elephant rescue organization, I decided to volunteer at an animal shelter.

 GRAMMAR

Underline the sentence adverbs in these conversations. Then write them in the chart below.

1. Jack: I don't trust all the facts in this documentary about Coco Chanel.
   Lisa: I don't agree. The writer <u>clearly</u> did his research and interviewed many people who knew her.

2. Jill: When is your new film coming out?
   Fei: Apparently in May, but there will be a private viewing in April.

3. Aaron: I wanted to see the new documentary about a homeless family, but it isn't playing anywhere.
   Emma: Haven't you heard? It was removed from the theaters. Supposedly, the director used footage of certain people without asking permission, and now there's a lawsuit.

4. Kurt: I'm surprised. That new action movie was so dull!
   Teresa: I know. The director probably thinks he doesn't need to try very hard after so many successful movies.

5. Josh: This is the third science fiction movie I've seen this month!
   Tara: Obviously, you really like that kind of movie.

6. Kazuo: This director's films are so funny!
   Julie: Yes, but unquestionably, there's a lot of deep emotion in them as well.

Certainty	Less certainty	Possibility and probability
clearly		

3 GRAMMAR

Rewrite these sentences using the sentence adverbs in parentheses.

1. That famous Dutch actor is going to direct a movie. (apparently)

   Apparently, that famous Dutch actor is going to direct a movie.

   That famous Dutch actor is apparently going to direct a movie.

2. Some movie studios are not interested in good acting as much as extreme action. (frankly)

   _____

3. This is a magazine for anyone with a very strong interest in cinema. (definitely)

   _____

4. There would be more interest in historical movies if they received more publicity. (probably)

   _____

5. Because of a lack of funding, fewer independent films will be made this year. (potentially)

   _____

4 GRAMMAR

How does watching movies in theaters compare with watching movies at home?
Write sentences using the adverbs provided.

1. *Watching a movie at home* is clearly *more comfortable than watching a movie in a theater.*

2. _____ is potentially _____

   _____

3. Overall, _____

   _____

4. _____ unquestionably the most _____

   _____

5. Unfortunately, _____

   _____

5 WRITING

A Choose either a comedy or a documentary that you are familiar with, and write a review of the movie you have chosen. Your review should answer the following questions.

Documentary

1. What is the title of the documentary?
2. What is the documentary mainly about?
3. What is the primary purpose of the documentary? Does it try to explain, persuade, or something else?
4. How successful is the documentary at achieving its purpose? Explain.
5. Which aspects of the documentary are especially memorable?
6. Would you recommend it to others? Why or why not?

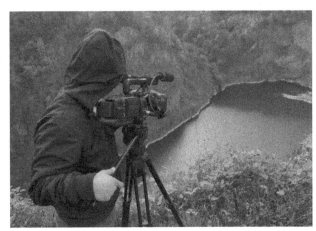

Comedy

1. What is the title of the comedy?
2. Who are the actors, and what characters do they play?
3. What is the basic plot of the movie?
4. What are the best aspects of the movie? Explain.
5. Is the movie successful as a comedy? Why or why not?
6. Would you recommend it to others? Why or why not?

_____

_____

_____

_____

_____

_____

_____

_____

_____

_____

_____

_____

B Read your review again. Are there places where adding more details would make your writing better? If so, go back and add these details.

GRAMMAR

Complete the email with *so*, *such*, *so many*, *so few*, *so much*, or *so little*.

To: nataliem3@cup.com
Subject: House

Hey Natalie,

Have you ever seen the TV show *House*? The series ended a while ago, but it's
1 ___such___ a good show that I can't stop watching the reruns! It's about a cranky doctor
and his medical team who save the lives of patients with mysterious diseases. I usually
have **2** _____ time for TV that I skip most medical dramas. But this show isn't a typical
medical drama where doctors are compassionate and
caring. Dr. House is rude. In fact, he's **3** _____ rude
that his patients are often afraid of him. But he's also
4 _____ a brilliant doctor that everybody admires
him. He knows **5** _____ about rare diseases that
he's usually the only person who can cure these patients.
I had no idea there were **6** _____ different kinds
of illnesses. I think you'd like this show. There are
7 _____ good shows on TV these days that you'll
really appreciate this one.

Marcus

VOCABULARY

Write the type of TV show next to its description.

cartoon	documentary	news program	sketch comedy show	sports program
cooking show	game show	sitcom	soap opera	talk show

___game show___   1. Participants compete for money and prizes by answering
questions that an average fifth grade student would know.

_____   2. The complicated lives of the wealthy Ramirez family are
dramatized daily.

_____   3. Ann Brady reports on the top news stories of the day.

_____   4. The Lakers take on the Suns in game three of the playoffs.

_____   5. Ty Ott interviews actor Ash Lake and chef Ami Tran.

_____   6. Astronaut Neil Armstrong's life is reviewed in this program.

_____   7. A boy and his ladybug friend star in this animated kids' show.

_____   8. Alice Lee stars in this funny half-hour show about high school.

_____   9. To win, chefs live together and prepare dishes for celebrity judges.

_____   10. Weekly guests star with the regular cast in a series of ridiculous
situations.

3 GRAMMAR

Write six logical sentences by choosing one word or phrase from each column.
Sometimes more than one answer is possible.

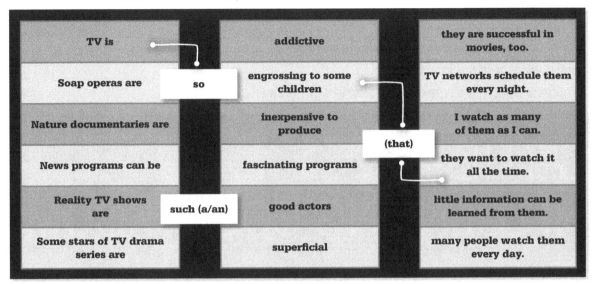

1. _TV is so engrossing to some children (that) they want to watch it all the time._
2. _____
3. _____
4. _____
5. _____
6. _____

4 GRAMMAR

Complete these sentences with your own ideas.

1. Some crime drama series can be so _violent_ that _I don't think children should_
   watch them.

2. There are so many _____ to watch this season that I
   _____

3. _____ is such a great actor that I _____
   _____

4. _____ night is such a good night to watch TV that _____
   _____

5. There are so few really funny shows on TV that I _____
   _____

6. Reality shows can be so _____ that I _____
   _____

A Read the article. Find the words in boldface that match these definitions.

1. legal officials who accuse someone of a crime   *prosecutors*
2. disqualify _____
3. scientific techniques used to investigate a crime _____
4. based on data rather than theory _____
5. groups of people who make a decision in a court case _____

IS THE "CSI EFFECT" INFLUENCING COURTROOMS?

The fictional forensic investigators in shows like *CSI: Crime Scene Investigation* put old-time detectives like Sherlock Holmes to shame. They can read a crime scene like it's a glossy magazine. But many **prosecutors** complain that shows like *CSI* make their job harder by creating the expectation that every trial must feature high-tech **forensic tests**. Some fear that when they don't show off *CSI*-style technology, **juries** might let criminals get away. It's termed the "*CSI* effect."

"I think that *CSI* has done some great things," says Mike Murphy, the coroner for Clark County, Nevada, whose office was the model for the original *CSI* show. "It's also caused some problems. And some of those problems are [that] people expect us to have DNA back in 20 minutes or that we're supposed to solve a crime in 60 minutes with three commercials. It doesn't happen that way," he says. Legal experts are concerned that juries may well be confusing fact with fiction.

However, Donald Shelton, the chief judge of Washtenaw County, Michigan, is skeptical. After realizing no **empirical** research on the *CSI* effect had been done, Shelton conducted a study showing that while jurors do expect to see scientific evidence in murder cases, their expectations have nothing to do with the TV shows they watch. They're more likely to be affected by the technology in their own pocket. "The more sophisticated [the] technological devices that jurors had, the higher their expectations for the prosecutors to present evidence," Shelton says.

Despite the lack of empirical evidence, lawyers, judges, and investigators act as if the *CSI* effect is real. In the U.S., some states now allow lawyers to **strike** potential jurors based on their TV habits. Judges are issuing instructions that warn juries about expecting too much scientific evidence based on what they see on TV. And in the field, Shelton says, investigators sometimes run useless tests just to show they went the extra *CSI* mile.

B Read these statements. Are they supported by the information in the article? Choose yes or no.

	Yes	No
1. Real or not, the *CSI* effect is clearly having an influence on courtrooms.	☐	☐
2. Shows like *CSI* definitely raise the expectations of jurors.	☐	☐
3. *CSI* realistically depicts how criminal investigations are conducted.	☐	☐
4. Some investigators now conduct tests only to impress juries.	☐	☐

6 MUSICIANS AND MUSIC

LESSON A ▶ *A world of music*

 GRAMMAR

Choose the words that best complete the sentences.

1. Generally, the more well known a singer is, the (more) / *less* money he or she makes.
2. The less publicity a musician gets, the *easier* / *harder* it is to make a living.
3. Some say the earlier you expose children to classical music, the *more* / *fewer* likely they are to excel in school.
4. The more relaxing the music, the *faster* / *slower* I fall asleep.
5. In my opinion, the more you listen to some song lyrics, the *fewer* / *less* you are able to understand them.
6. For some musicians, the more people gossip about their private lives, the *better* / *sooner*!

 GRAMMAR

Complete the interview with the words from the box.

better	less	longer	more	sooner

Lily: When did you realize you wanted to be a guitarist?

Shane: I was 10 years old. My brother was taking guitar lessons, and the more I heard him practice, the (1) _____*more*_____ I wanted to play guitar just as well.

Lily: Who were your biggest musical influences?

Shane: My biggest influence was Jack White. The more I listened to his music, the (2) _____ it got.

Lily: Jack White is great, but your music doesn't sound like his.

Shane: Yeah, I know. I realized that the more I listened to Jack White's music, the (3) _____ I wanted to sound like him. I wanted my own sound – something that made me unique.

Lily: You've certainly succeeded! What's next for you?

Shane: I'm moving to New York City. The (4) _____ I stay in Los Angeles, the more I realize I need a change.

Lily: Why is that?

Shane: I'd like to be part of a growing music scene, and apparently a lot is happening in New York.

Lily: When will you leave?

Shane: I'm not sure yet, but I think the (5) _____ I leave, the better.

3 VOCABULARY

Choose the adjectives that best describe your opinion of each kind of music. Then write a sentence explaining why.

1. pop (catchy / frenetic / monotonous)

   Successful pop music is catchy. The best pop songs are
   hard to forget — even years later.

2. classical (exhilarating / haunting / soothing)

   _____

   _____

3. jazz (evocative / mellow / frenetic)

   _____

   _____

4. hip-hop (catchy / evocative / monotonous)

   _____

   _____

5. folk (haunting / soothing / catchy)

   _____

   _____

6. rock (monotonous / exhilarating / frenetic)

   _____

   _____

4 GRAMMAR

Complete the sentences with double comparatives and your own ideas to make them true for you.

1. The _____ *louder* _____ the music, the _____ *more* _____ I like it.

2. The _____ the lyrics of a song, the more likely I am to

   _____.

3. The _____ the music, the _____ I find it.

4. The _____ a musician's reputation, the _____
   I am to go to his or her concerts.

5. The _____ a piece of music, the more difficult it is to

   _____.

6. The _____ musicians use _____ in their songs,
   the less I enjoy them.

 **WRITING**

A Read the characteristics of listening to live music and listening to recorded music. Then put them under the correct heading below.

> You listen with many other people.
> Sometimes you hear music you don't like.
> You can't see the musicians while you listen.
> You can sing along with your favorite songs.
> You can adjust the volume.
> You can hear music by well-known artists.
>
> You can't adjust the volume.
> You can listen to a song over and over.
> You can listen to any kind of music you're in the mood for.
> You can listen to music in any order you'd like.
> You can turn off or skip songs you don't like.
> You can listen only when musicians are playing on stage.

Live music

_____

_____

_____

_____

_____

_____

Recorded music

_____

_____

_____

_____

_____

_____

Live music and recorded music

_____

_____

_____

_____

_____

_____

B What is your opinion of listening to live music versus listening to recorded music? Write a thesis statement expressing your opinion on the subject.

_____

_____

_____

C Now write a compare-and-contrast essay. Include your thesis statement in the introduction, two paragraphs describing the similarities and differences, and a conclusion restating your point of view.

LESSON B ▶ *Getting your big break*

1 VOCABULARY

Correct the underlined mistake in each sentence with one of the words in the box.
Some words will be used more than once.

| be | break | get | make | pay |

1. Most musicians must <u>break</u> their dues before they become successful. _____*pay*_____

2. After retiring in 2012, my favorite band is planning to <u>get</u> a comeback. _____

3. Gotye's latest song is going to <u>pay</u> a big hit. _____

4. I want to be a singer. What advice do you have to <u>make</u> into the business? _____

5. Many famous singers <u>be</u> their big break as contestants on *American Idol*. _____

6. It was so difficult for Jay-Z to <u>break</u> his foot in the door that he started his own record label. _____

7. The first time I heard Madonna, I knew she wouldn't <u>pay</u> a one-hit wonder. _____

8. While some musicians may be talented and work hard, they might never <u>get</u> a name for themselves in the music industry. _____

2 GRAMMAR

Complete these conversations. Use the verbs in parentheses and *would* or *will*.

1. Kim: I used to listen to all kinds of music when I was younger.
   Ron: Not me! When I was young, I _____*would listen*_____ (listen) only to rock music.

2. Dan: You play the guitar so well. How often do you practice?
   Sally: I practice all the time. In fact, I _____ (practice) four to five hours a day, depending on my schedule.

3. Mario: What do you like to do in your spare time?
   Kate: I don't have much spare time, but when I do, I _____ (go) to jazz clubs and concerts. Music helps me relax.

4. Fay: I can't believe the lead singer of the band we saw spent so much time after the show talking with his fans and signing autographs.
   Amy: I know. Most singers these days _____ (not spend) any time with their fans, let alone sign autographs!

5. Paula: When I was a teenager, I loved to listen to music that was really loud.
   Diana: Me, too. In fact, I _____ (turn up) my stereo as loud as I could. Unfortunately, now I have hearing problems.

6. Rob: I just heard my favorite Beatles song on the radio.
   Lori: I love the Beatles. In college I _____ (listen) to them every day.

3 GRAMMAR

Read the sentences about a band. Then choose the sentences that incorrectly use *will* or *would* and correct them.

☑ 1. When the band comes onstage, the crowd would scream.
   When the band comes onstage, the crowd will scream.

☐ 2. Before the band got so popular, it will never sell out a concert in such a short time.
   _____

☐ 3. Years ago, only bands with great musicianship would make it big.
   _____

☐ 4. When the guitarist was young, he would practice in front of a mirror.
   _____

☐ 5. In the past, the band will play only hard rock songs.
   _____

☐ 6. Although the band used to sign autographs after a show, these days, security guards would not let fans backstage.
   _____

4 GRAMMAR

Which music habits were or were not true for you in the past? Which are or are not true now? Write sentences with *would* or *will*.

1. listen to a song over and over again
   When I find a song I really love, I will listen to it over
   and over again.

2. listen to very loud music
   _____
   _____

3. spend a lot of money downloading music
   _____
   _____

4. take music lessons
   _____
   _____

5. travel long distances to see live concerts of favorite bands
   _____

6. argue with family members about musical tastes
   _____

A Read the article quickly. What do you think the root *neuro-* in words such as *neurobiologist* means?

Music May Someday Help Repair the Brain

The music that makes the foot tap, the fingers snap, and the pulse quicken stirs the brain at its most fundamental levels, suggesting that scientists one day may be able to retune damaged minds by exploiting rhythm, harmony, and melody, according to some research.

"Undeniably, there is a biology of music," said neurobiologist Mark Jude Tramo. "Music is biologically part of human life, just as music is aesthetically part of human life."

Researchers found that the brain:

■ Responds directly to harmony. Neuroscientists discovered that different parts of the brain involved in emotion are activated depending on whether the music is pleasant or unpleasant.

■ Interprets written music in an area on its right side. That region corresponds to an area on the opposite side of the brain known to handle written words and letters. So, researchers uncovered an anatomical link between music and language.

■ Grows in response to musical training. In a study of classically trained musicians, researchers discovered that male musicians have significantly larger brains than men who have not had extensive musical training. Although no similar increase has been found in female musicians, this might be explained by insufficient and inconclusive research.

Overall, music seems to involve the brain at almost every level, and researchers are already looking for ways to harness the power of music to change the brain. Research also suggests that music may play some role in enhancing intelligence. Indeed, so seductive is the possibility that music can boost a child's IQ that some politicians have lobbied for children to be exposed regularly to Mozart sonatas, although such research has yet to be confirmed.

The scientists said the research could help the clinical practice of neurology, including cognitive rehabilitation. As a therapeutic tool, for example, some doctors already use music to help rehabilitate stroke patients. Surprisingly, some stroke patients who have lost their ability to speak retain their ability to sing, and that opens an avenue for therapists to retrain the brain's speech centers.

B Read the statements. Are they supported by the information in the article? Choose yes or no.

	Yes	No
1. Different areas of the brain respond to music.	☐	☐
2. The brains of classically trained male musicians grow larger than the brains of nonmusical males.	☐	☐
3. Different pieces of classical music affect the brain in different ways.	☐	☐
4. Children who listen to Mozart sonatas develop higher intelligence than those who do not have exposure to this music.	☐	☐
5. Some stroke victims who are unable to speak are able to sing.	☐	☐